In Search of Sharks
HUGE SHARKS

David Thompson

PowerKiDS press
New York

Published in 2022 by The Rosen Publishing Group, Inc.
29 East 21st Street, New York, NY 10010

Originally Published in English by Haynes Publishing under the title: Sharks Pocket Manual © Haynes Publishing 2019

All rights reserved. No part of this book may be reproduced in any form without permission in writing from the publisher, except by a reviewer.

Cataloging-in-Publication Data
Names: Thompson, David.
Title: Huge sharks / David Thompson.
Description: New York : PowerKids Press, 2022. | Series: In search of sharks | Includes glossary and index.
Identifiers: ISBN 9781725332638 (pbk.) | ISBN 9781725332652 (library bound) | ISBN 9781725332645 (6 pack) | ISBN 9781725332669 (ebook)
Subjects: LCSH: Sharks--Juvenile literature.
Classification: LCC QL638.9 T466 2022 | DDC 597.3--dc23

Design by Richard Parsons and James Robertson

The following agencies have given permission to use their images:

Cover, Wildestanimal/Alamy Stock Photo; Cover, p. 1, 30-32 Alexander Tolstykh/Shutterstock.com; Erika Yves Antoniazzo: p164; Dray van Beeck: p42, 86, 88, 118-124, 150, 168; Dan Bolt: p154, 156; Paul vander Eecken: p62-68; David B. Fleetham: p34-40, 114, 116; Saul Gonor/seapics.com: p84; Daniel W. Gotshall/seapics.com: p128; Marion Haarsma: p60; Tom Haught/seapics.com: p102; Dean Innell: p172; Dennis King: p18, 20; Gwen Lowe/seapics.com: p54, 56; Randy Morse: p110, 112; Andy Murch: p12, 52, 76, 138, 140, 180; Doug Perrine/seapics.com: p178; Bruce Rasna/seapics.com: p104; David Shen/seapics.com: p70, 72; Marty Snyderman/seapics.com: p130, 132; David Thompson: p16, 24, 30, 32, 96, 100, 102, 104, 108, 136, 144, 152, 182, 184; Cary Yany: 160; Murat Zayim: p176

Manufactured in the United States of America

CPSIA Compliance Information: Batch #CWPK22. For further information contact Rosen Publishing, New York, New York at 1-800-237-9932.

Contents

Shark Anatomy	4
Basking Shark	6
Bluntnose Sixgill Shark	8
Great Hammerhead	10
Great White Shark	12
Greenland Shark	14
Manta Ray	16
Megamouth Shark	18
Spotted Ragged-Tooth	22
Whale Shark	24
Zebra Shark	26
Glossary	30
For More Information	31
Index	32

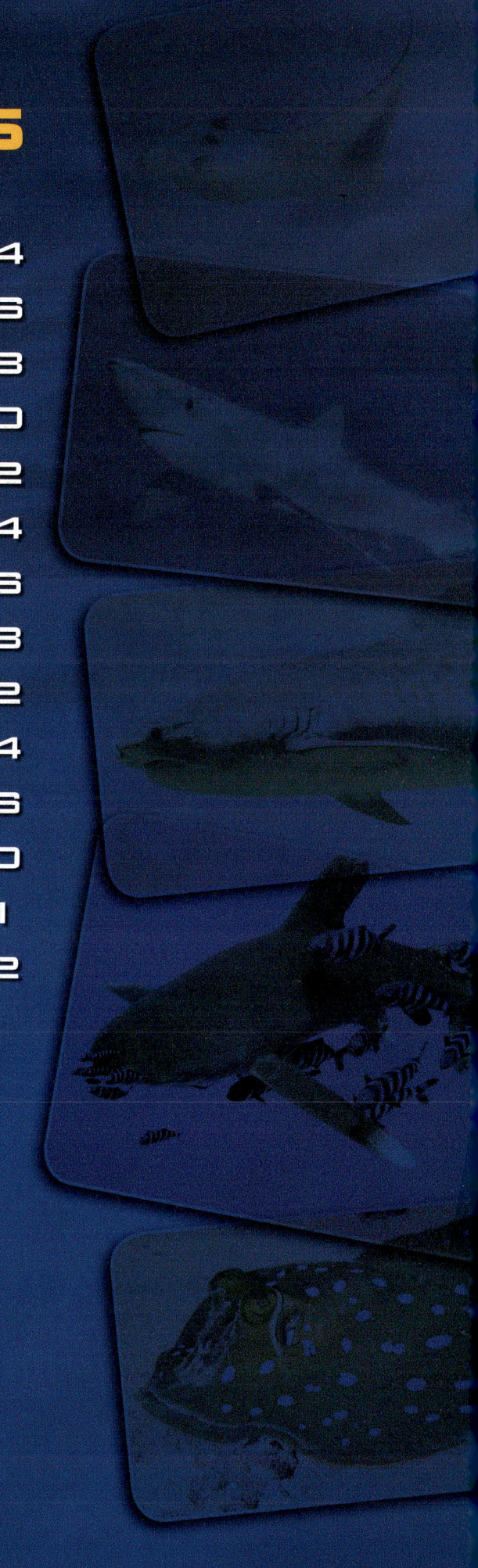

Shark Anatomy

An introduction

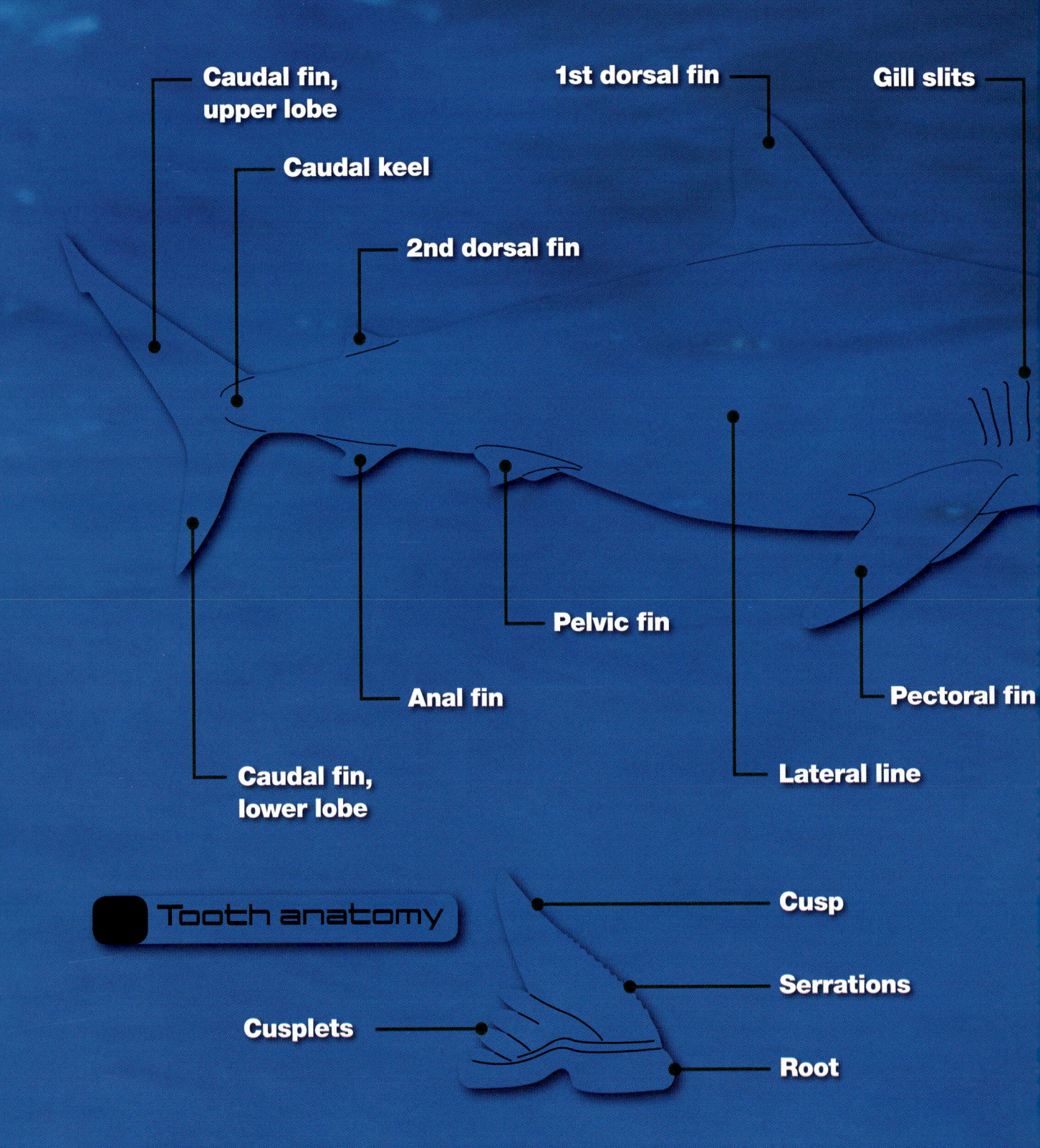

Caudal fin, upper lobe

Caudal keel

2nd dorsal fin

1st dorsal fin

Gill slits

Pelvic fin

Anal fin

Pectoral fin

Caudal fin, lower lobe

Lateral line

Tooth anatomy

Cusp

Serrations

Cusplets

Root

4

Scientific terminology

Reproduction

Oviparous	Shark lays egg cases that hatch independently from the mother
Ovoviviparous	Shark produces eggs, which remain inside the body, where they hatch
Uterine cannibalism	The first pups to develop or hatch eat the remaining eggs/embryos or other pups in the womb
Viviparous	Shark gives birth to live pups that have developed inside the womb

Taxonomy

Batoids	Flat fish closley related to sharks, also known as rays or "flat sharks"
Bony fish	All fish other than sharks and rays
Cephalopods	Octopus and squid
Crustaceans	Crabs, lobsters, prawns, and shrimps
Invertebrates	Animals without a backbone
Mollusks	Mussels, snails, and other snail-like animals that live in a shell

Habitat

Benthic	Lives on the bottom of the sea either on or in the sediment/sand
Continental shelf	The shallow depths around the coasts of continents, which can extend many miles out to sea
Pelagic	Open-ocean dwelling

Mouth

Eye and spiracle behind

Nostril

Snout

Basking Shark
Cetorhinus maximus

The second-largest shark, the basking shark has a huge mouth and gill slits that almost surround the head. It has a pointed snout and tiny hooked teeth. It filters plankton on the surface at tidal water fronts and relies on movement to push the plankton through its gills. Basking sharks often swim together in intricate patterns when feeding and sometimes they spring entirely out of the water, called breaching, to try to dislodge parasites. They are found in cold to warm coastal waters but migrate to deeper, offshore waters in winter. The female produces a large number of eggs inside her, which hatch gradually, and the first hatchlings then eat the remaining eggs (uterine cannibalism) but not each other. Basking sharks are harmless to humans and will approach boats without fear.

Statistics

Common name	Basking shark
Family	Basking sharks
Size at birth	Likely 5–6 feet (1.5–1.8 m)
Maximum size	40 feet (12 m)
Maximum weight	10,000 pounds (4,500 kg)
Maturity at	Male: 13–23 feet (4–7 m) Female: 25–33 feet (8–10 m)
Reproduction	Ovoviviparous with uterine cannibalism
Litter size	1–6
Food	Plankton, krill, and possibly other small fish
Top speed	2.5 miles (4 km) per hour
Teeth count	1,000+
Depth	0–6,500 feet (0–2,000 m)

Geographic distribution ■ Confirmed ■ Possible

Bluntnose Sixgill Shark

Hexanchus griseus

This is a very large, stocky, broad-headed sixgill shark, with only one dorsal fin close to the tail and an extra-long upper lobe of the tail. The teeth are blade-like and shaped like the crest on a rooster's head, becoming smaller at the back of the jaw. The lower jaw teeth are larger than the upper jaw teeth, which are smaller and more pointed. It also has long pointed teeth in the upper front row. This shark is found worldwide in temperate to tropical deep-sea waters off coastal and island shelves. It appears to be very sensitive to light, staying in the dark murky depths during the day and only coming up to the shallows to feed at night. It eats fish, sharks, rays, squid, seals, crustaceans, and carrion. Although no attacks on humans have been reported, young bluntnose sixgills will snap at fishermen when hooked on fishing lines. Adults, however, will remain calm.

Statistics

Common name	Bluntnose sixgill shark
Family	Cow sharks
Size at birth	23–30 inches (60–75 cm)
Maximum size	18 feet (5.5 m)
Maximum weight	1,300 pounds (590 kg)
Maturity at	Male: 13–15 feet (4–4.5 m) Female: 14.5–16 feet (4.4–4.9 m)
Reproduction	Ovoviviparous
Litter size	100–110
Food	Fish, sharks, rays, squid, seals, crustaceans, and carrion
Top speed	Unknown
Teeth count	26–30
Depth	0 to at least 6,135 feet (0–1,870 m)

Geographic distribution ■ Confirmed ■ Possible

Great Hammerhead

Sphyrna mokarran

This hammerhead is easily recognized as a very large shark with a huge first dorsal fin and an almost straight front edge to its hammer, which is extended far in front of its gills. The front teeth are long and broad with heavily serrated edges and the back teeth are almost molar-shaped. It is found worldwide in tropical coastal and semi-oceanic waters, preferring continental and island coral reefs, although it appears to move toward the poles in the summer. It feeds on rays, batoid fish, fish, squid, and other sharks. It seems to be immune to the stings from stingrays – one was found with more than 50 stings stuck in its mouth and tongue! Although not an agressive shark, the great hammerhead is dangerous because it is fearless and eats almost anything.

Statistics

Common name	Great (or giant) hammerhead shark
Family	Hammerhead sharks
Size at birth	20–28 inches (50–70 cm)
Maximum size	18–20 feet (5.5–6.2 m)
Maximum weight	990 pounds (450 kg)
Maturity at	Male: 7.5–9 feet (2.3–2.7 m) Female: 8.2–9.8 feet (2.5–3 m)
Reproduction	Viviparous
Litter size	13–42
Food	Fish, squid, octopus, rays and other batoids, other sharks
Top speed	25 miles (40 km) per hour
Teeth count	69–80
Depth	0–260 feet (0–80 m)

Geographic distribution ■ Confirmed ■ Possible

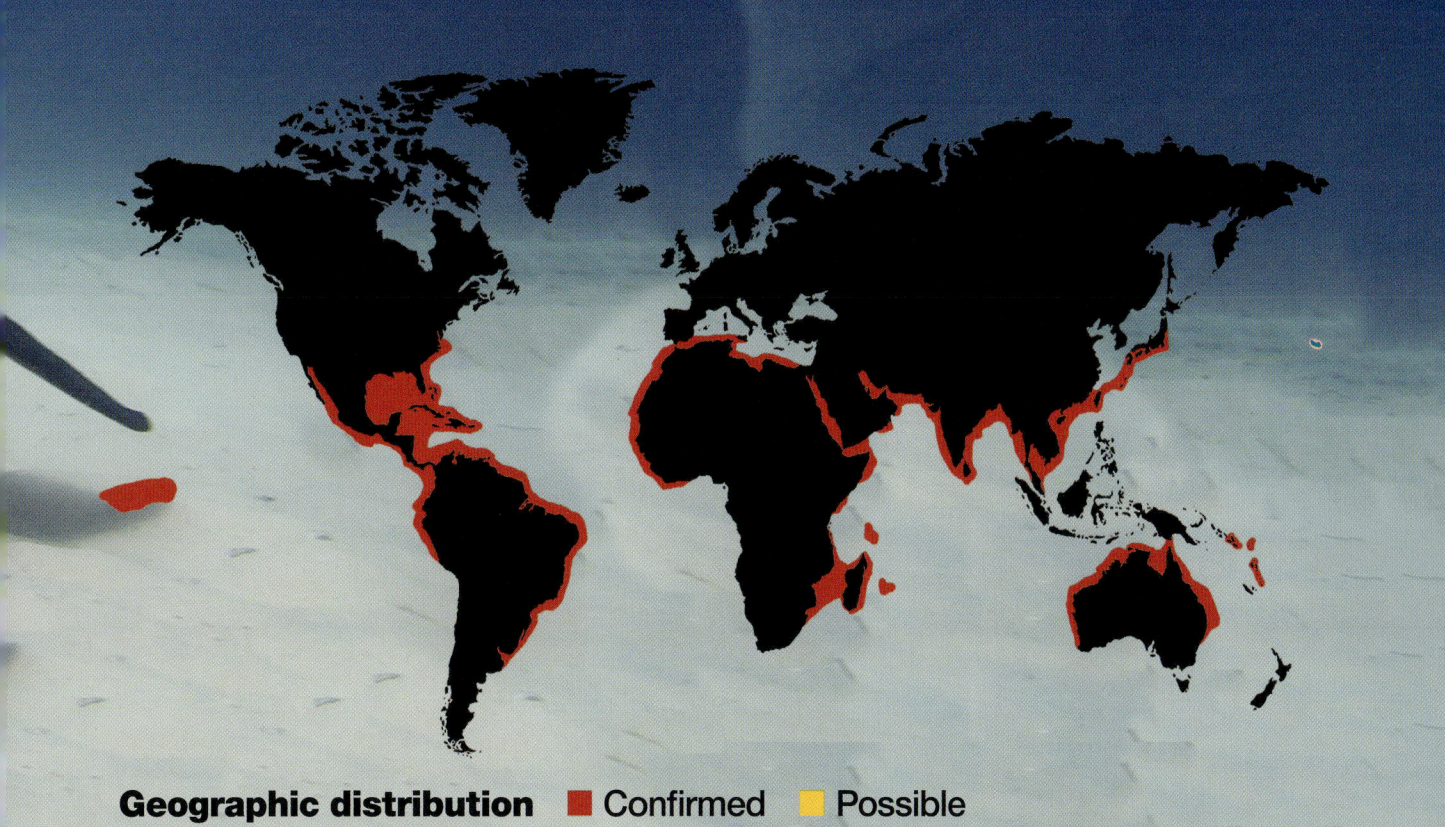

Great White Shark

Carcharodon carcharias

This is a huge spindle-shaped shark with a white belly and a gray to blackish-gray upper body. It has a long pointed snout and very distinctive black eyes. The teeth are large, flat, triangular, and saw-like with serrated edges. The great white can be found in most waters worldwide, but mostly in cooler temperate waters. It prefers coasts and offshore islands, but has also been spotted in the open ocean. It is an active swimmer, usually cruising at about 1 to 2 miles (1.6–3.2 km) per hour. However, it will sometimes produce very fast sprints and even spring completely out of the water. It eats marine mammals (including small whales), reptiles, birds, sharks, fish, crustaceans, and squid. The female produces 2–14 egg cases, which hatch inside her, and uterine cannibalism is common. The mother stops eating during the pupping period so as not to eat her own young. The great white is number one in the shark attack files, although it is more likely that most attacks were by the tiger shark.

Statistics

Common name	Great white shark
Family	Mackerel sharks
Size at birth	3.6–5.6 feet (1.1–1.7 m)
Maximum size	20–23 feet (6–7 m)
Maximum weight	7,500 pounds (3,400 kg)
Maturity at	Male: 11.5–13.5 feet (3.5–4.1 m) Female: 13–16.5 feet (4–5 m)
Reproduction	Ovoviviparous
Litter size	2–14
Food	Marine mammals, reptiles, birds, fish, crustaceans, sharks, and carrion
Top speed	25 miles (40 km) per hour
Teeth count	50–60
Depth	0–4,200 feet (0–1,280 m)

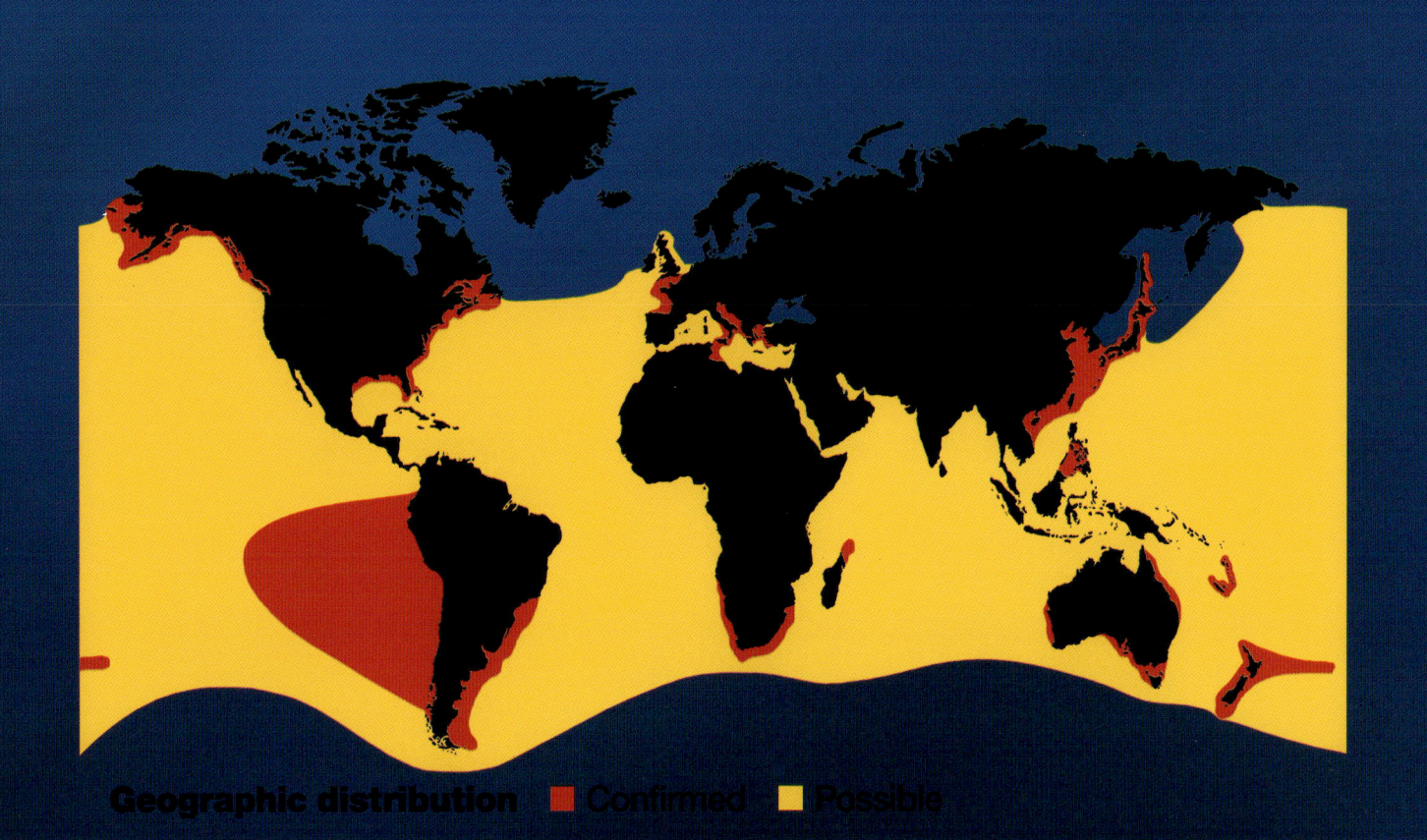

Geographic distribution   ■ Confirmed   ■ Possible

Greenland Shark

Somniosus microcephalus

The Greenland shark is a large, sluggish shark with a short snout, cylindrical body, and no anal fins. The dorsal fins are very small, spineless, and positioned far back on the body. The teeth are spear-shaped in the upper jaw, and short and broad with oblique cusps in the lower jaw. All of the teeth are razor sharp and are sometimes used by people as knives. It is found in cold Arctic and North Atlantic waters from the shallows down to at least 4,100 feet (1,250 m). It has a unique copepod parasite (a shrimplike animal) attached to each eye that glows in the dark. These are believed to attract fish so the shark can catch them. It eats almost anything, but its main diet is fish, although it will eat marine mammals and any carrion it can find. It is considered harmless to humans, although there are some stories of it attacking boats.

Statistics

Common name	Greenland shark
Family	Sleeper sharks
Size at birth	14.5 inches (37 cm)
Maximum size	21–23 feet (6.5–7 m)
Maximum weight	1,710 pounds (776 kg)
Maturity at	Male: 11–12 feet (3.4–3.6 m) Female: 15.8–16.4 feet (4.8–5 m)
Reproduction	Ovoviviparous
Litter size	Approximately 10
Food	Fish, skates, seals, dead whales, and any other carrion
Top speed	At least 0.75 mile (1.2 km) per hour
Teeth count	98–104
Depth	0–4,100 feet (0–1,250 m)

Geographic distribution ■ Confirmed ■ Possible

Manta Ray
Manta birostris

Rays are not technically sharks, but they are closely related to them. In fact, they share so many similarities that they're sometimes called "flat sharks" by those who study them. The manta ray is the largest batoid or ray with a maximum "wing" span of 30 feet (9 m). Like other rays, the pectoral fins are fused to the head and form large triangular wings, but unlike other rays, the manta's mouth is at the front of the head instead of below. The tail is short and has no poisonous spines. It has two special fins, one on each side of the mouth that look like horns, to funnel plankton into its mouth. It has a brown to black upper body and a white belly. All mantas have different markings on both the back and the belly, which are as unique as fingerprints. It has only very small, nonfunctional teeth in the upper jaw, and eats plankton, krill, and some small fish. Manta rays are found worldwide in tropical waters, and they are harmless to humans.

Statistics

Common name	Manta ray or devil ray
Family	Devil rays
Size at birth	Disc width of 3.3–4 feet (1–1.2 m) wide
Maximum size	13 feet (4 m) long (without the tail), 30 feet (9 m) wide
Maximum weight	6,600 pounds (3,000 kg)
Maturity at	Male: Disc width of 13 feet (4 m) Female: Disc width of 16.5 feet (5 m)
Reproduction	Ovoviviparous
Litter size	1–2
Food	Plankton, krill, and very small fish
Top speed	22 miles (35 km) per hour
Teeth count	12–18 (lower jaw only)
Depth	0–165 feet (0–50 m)

Geographic distribution ■ Confirmed ■ Possible

Megamouth Shark
Megachasma pelagios

This is a huge and distinctive shark with a short, broad snout and a very large black mouth. The insides of the gills have "rakers" (netlike filters) for filtering plankton. The mouth is believed to be luminous, attracting shrimp like a light trap, and has lots of small, hooked teeth. The body is very flabby and is prone to attacks from the cookie-cutter shark. This is a very rare shark and only approximately 20 specimens have been found, but it is thought to live in warm, deep waters, moving from deep water during the day to shallower water at night. Very little is known about its habits and it is believed only to eat small shrimp, krill, jellyfish, and plankton. It is totally harmless to humans.

Statistics

Common name	Megamouth shark
Family	Megamouth sharks
Size at birth	Unknown
Maximum size	16–20 feet (5–6 m)
Maximum weight	7,700–8,800 pounds (3,500–4,000 kg)
Maturity at	Male: unknown Female: approx. 15.5 feet (4.7 m)
Reproduction	Viviparous
Litter size	Unknown but uterine cannibalism is suspected
Food	Plankton, krill, and other small shrimp
Top speed	1.3 miles (2.1 km) per hour
Teeth count	1,000+
Depth	16–15,000 feet (5–4,600 m)

Geographic distribution ■ Confirmed ■ Possible

The megamouth shark's name is fitting. A 16-foot-long (5 m) megamouth will likely have a mouth about 4 feet (1.2 m) across!

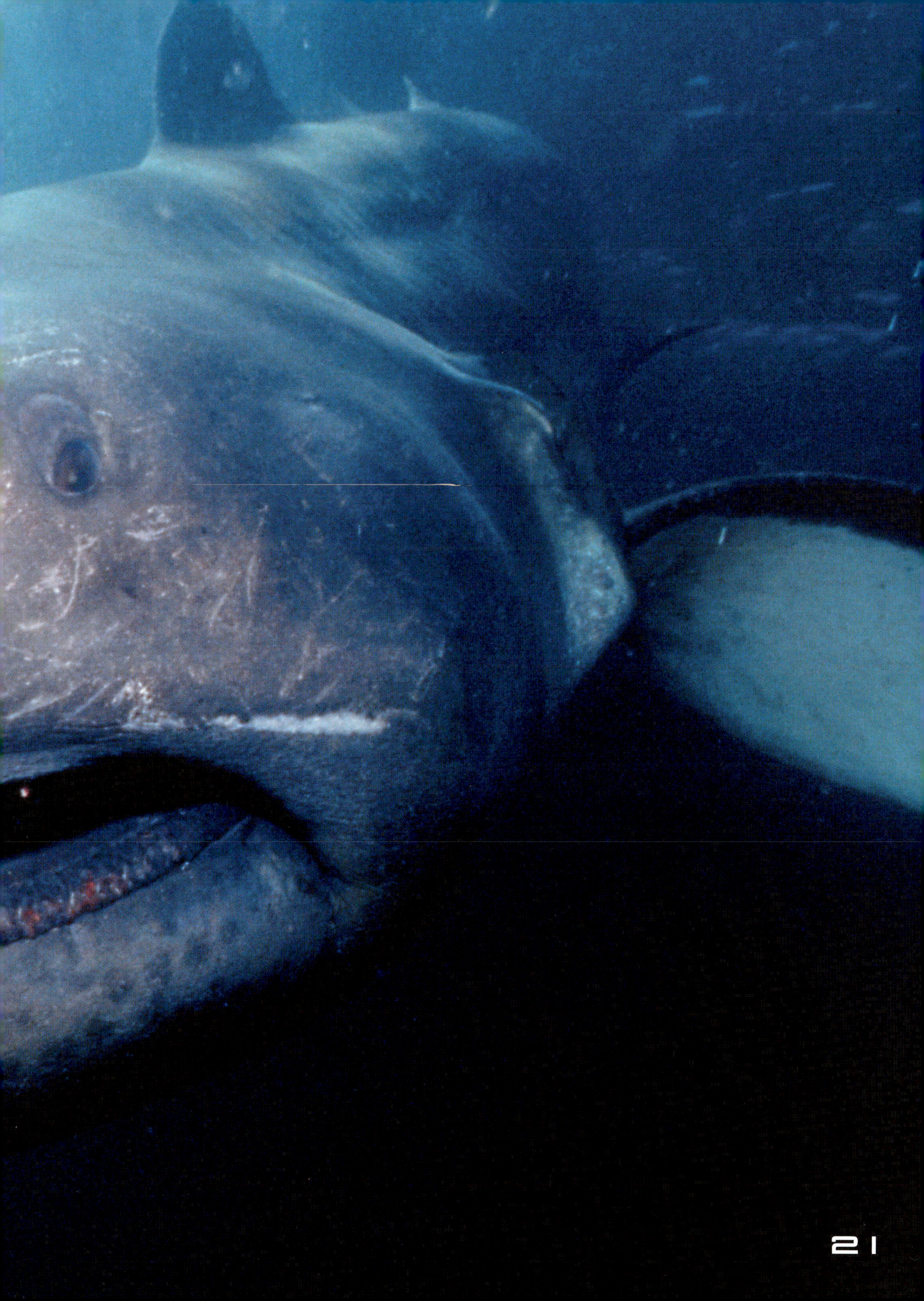

Spotted Ragged-Tooth

Carcharias taurus

This is a large and stocky light brown shark with reddish or dark brown spots. The snout is flattish and cone-shaped and the eyes are green. The teeth are long, pointed, and dagger-shaped with pointed cusplets to the side of the main tooth point, and stick out from the mouth. Although this shark is heavier than water it is able to "hover" very still in the water, just above the bottom, by gulping air into its stomach at the surface. It lives worldwide in warm temperate and tropical coastal waters, although not in the central and eastern Pacific, and is found either alone or in groups of 60–80. It eats fish, sharks, rays, cephalopods, crustaceans, and marine mammals. The female produces 15–25 eggs and uterine cannibalism occurs, resulting in only two pups being born. This is the most common shark to be found in large public aquariums and although harmless to humans, it may bite if annoyed.

Statistics

Common name	"Raggie" or spotted ragged-tooth shark
Family	Sand Tiger sharks
Size at birth	37–41 inches (94–105 cm)
Maximum size	10.5–14 feet (3.2–4.3 m)
Maximum weight	350 pounds (159 kg)
Maturity at	Male: 6.2–6.6 feet (1.9–2 m) Female: 7.2–8.2 feet (2.2–2.5 m)
Reproduction	Ovoviviparous
Litter size	2 live pups
Food	Fish, sharks, rays, cephalopods, crustaceans, and marine mammals
Top speed	20 miles (32 km) per hour
Teeth count	102–106
Depth	0 to at least 650 feet (0–200 m)

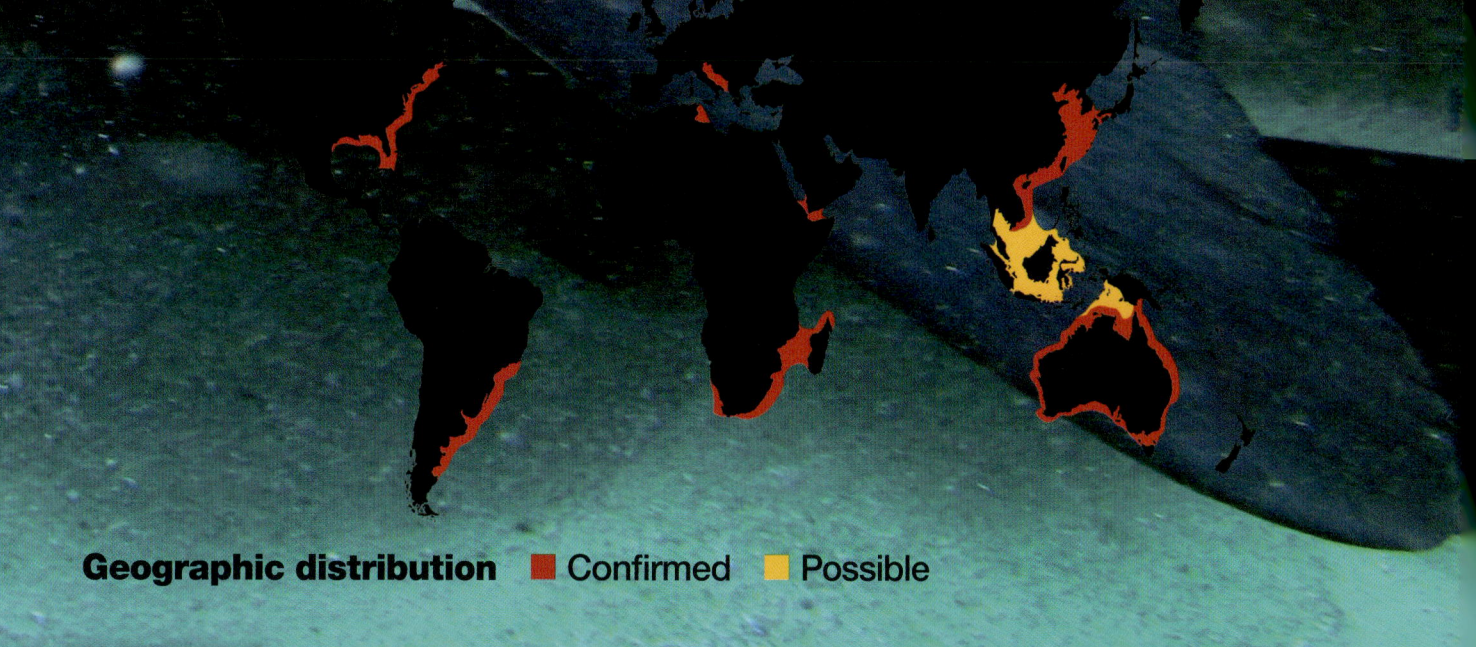

Geographic distribution ■ Confirmed ■ Possible

Whale Shark

Rhincodon typus

The whale shark is an unmistakable and extremely large gray shark with unique white dots and stripes on its body and fins. It has a large, broad head and mouth, which contains more than 300 rows of tiny teeth and gills that are much larger than normal, with extra filter screens on the inside slits. This is one of the three plankton-feeding sharks and is found worldwide in warm temperate and tropical, coastal, and oceanic waters and even coral reef lagoons. Generally, whale sharks swim just below the surface and they have been tagged and followed by satellites over distances of more than 2,175 miles (3,500 km) over a period of five months. This is a curious shark, approaching divers, snorkelers, and boats to "check them out." It is totally harmless to humans, although a bump from its tail will hurt!

Statistics

Common name	Whale shark
Family	Whale sharks
Size at birth	23–25 inches (58–64 cm)
Maximum size	53–60 feet (16–18 m)
Maximum weight	79,000 pounds (35,800 kg)
Maturity at	Male: 16–20 feet (5–6 m) Female: 20–26 feet (6–8 m)
Reproduction	Ovoviviparous
Litter size	Up to 300 in litter
Food	Plankton, krill, and other small fish
Top speed	6 miles (9.7 km) per hour
Teeth count	300+
Depth	0–2,300 feet (0–700 m)

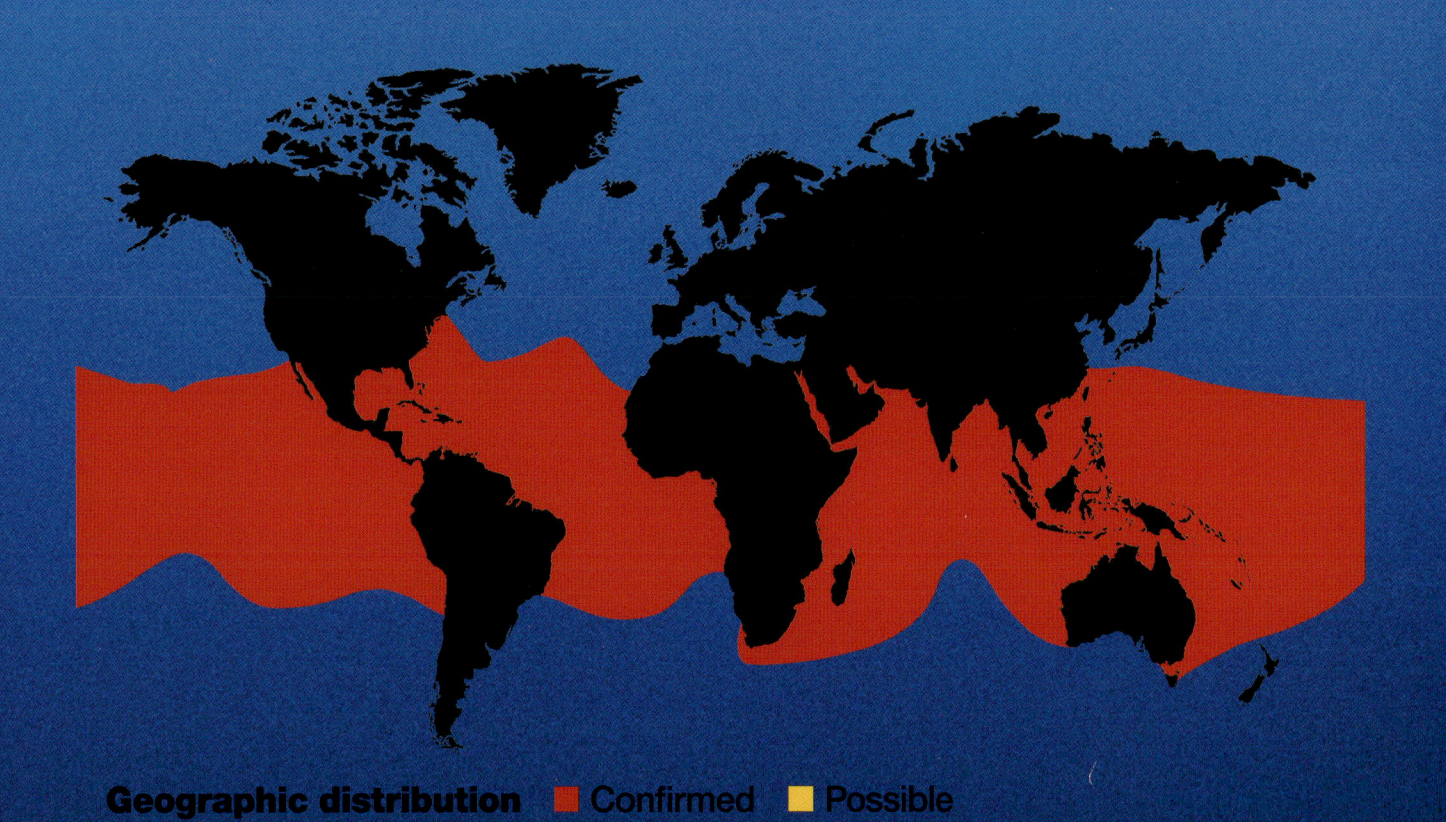

Geographic distribution ■ Confirmed ■ Possible

Zebra Shark
or Leopard Nurse Shark
Stegostoma fasciatum

This is a unique large shark, with a round body, ridges on its back, and a long tail almost the same length as the rest of the shark. It has nasal grooves with barbels on each side and a straight, narrow mouth. It is black with yellow zebra stripes when young and has a leopard-spotted coat when mature. It is found in tropical inshore waters of the west Indo-Pacific oceans, Australia, China, Japan, and west Asia. Its teeth are small and trident-shaped (three-pronged) with a tall, pointed cusp and two lateral pointed cusplets. It is generally found resting on the sand between corals facing the current in the day and is assumed to be more active during the night. It eats snails, mussels, crabs, shrimp, and small fish. The female lays one to four egg cases with hairlike tufts that anchor the case to the reef. It is harmless to humans. However, if annoyed, it will bite and then hold on like a bulldog. Climbing out of the water is difficult with a large shark attached to your leg!

Statistics

Common name	Zebra shark or leopard nurse shark
Family	Zebra sharks
Size at birth	8–14 inches (20–36 cm)
Maximum size	11.8 feet (3.6 m)
Maximum weight	475 pounds (215 kg)
Maturity at	Male: 5–6 feet (1.5–1.8 m) Female: 5.5–6 feet (1.7–1.8 m)
Reproduction	Oviparous
Litter size	1–4 egg cases
Food	Mollusks, crustaceans, and small bony fish
Top speed	Unknown
Teeth count	50–64
Depth	0 to at least 165 feet (0–50 m)

Geographic distribution ■ Confirmed ■ Possible

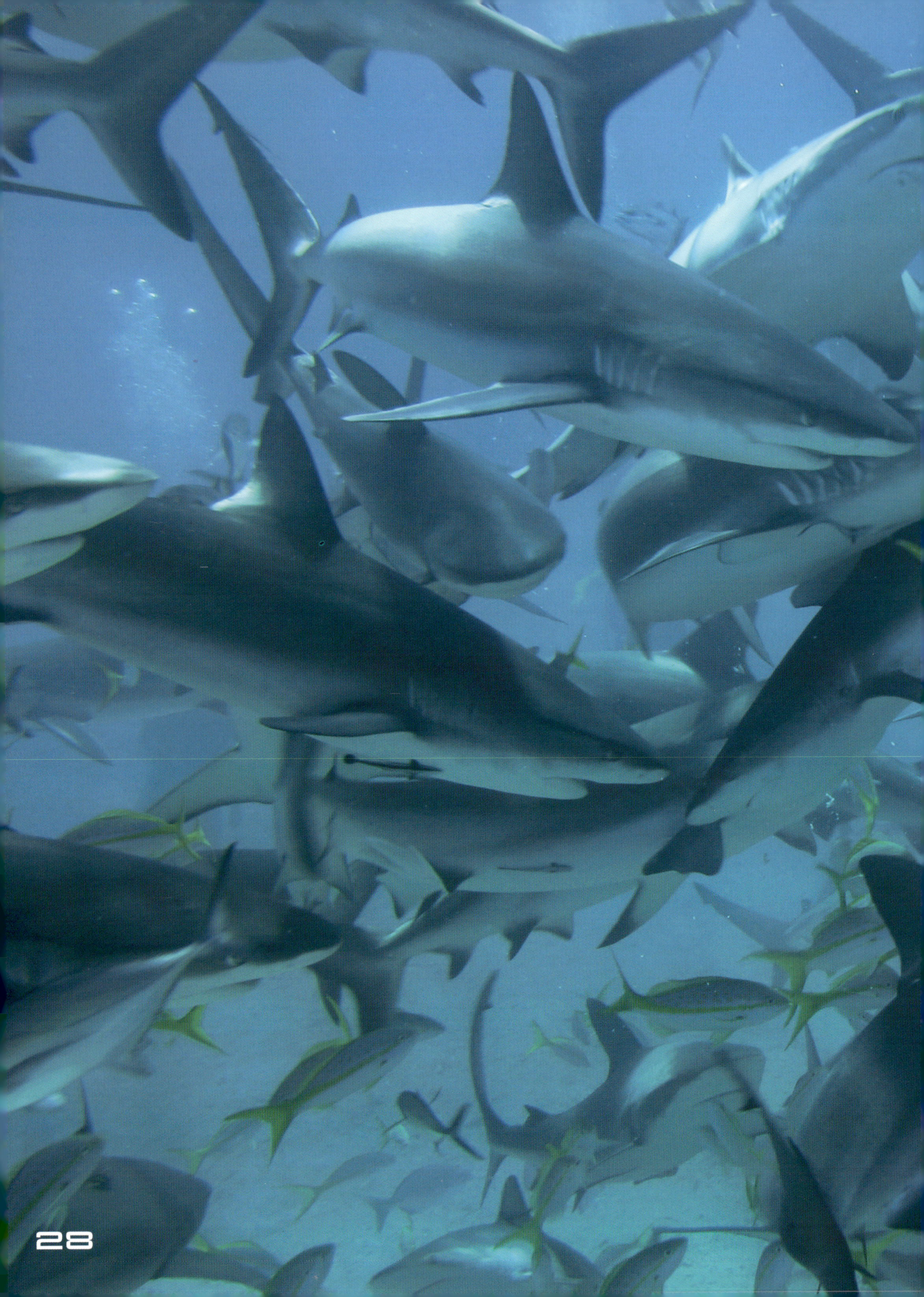

Feeding frenzy: Caribbean reef sharks, *Carcharhinus perezi*, attacking a frozen food ball.

GLOSSARY

anatomy: The parts that form a living thing.

carrion: A dead, rotting animal.

immune: Not affected by something, such as a disease or illness.

krill: A tiny marine creature that looks like a shrimp.

migrate: To move from one area to another for a season or for feeding or having babies.

oblique: Having a slanting or sloping direction.

parasite: A living thing that lives in, on, or with another living thing and often harms it.

plankton: A tiny plant or animal that floats in the ocean.

serrated: Having a row of small, sharp points or teeth like a saw.

spindle: Something shaped like a long, thin pole.

tropical: Having to do with the warm parts of Earth near the equator.

FOR MORE INFORMATION

Books

Jaycox, Jaclyn. *Great White Sharks*. North Mankato, MN: Pebble, 2020.

Kelly, Joni. *400-Year-Old Sharks!* New York, NY: Gareth Stevens Publishing, 2019.

Murray, Julie. *Hammerhead Sharks*. Minneapolis, MN: Big Buddy Books, an imprint of Abdo Publishing, 2020.

Websites

Great White Shark
kids.nationalgeographic.com/animals/fish/facts/great-white-shark
Read more about these giant predators and watch a video here.

Learn About Sharks
www.floridamuseum.ufl.edu/discover-fish/sharks/
This page from the Florida Museum of Natural History has links to help you learn more about all kinds of sharks, including the mighty megamouth shark!

Sharks
www.dkfindout.com/us/animals-and-nature/fish/sharks/
See what the inside of a shark looks like and learn even more about the fearsome fish on this interactive page.

Publisher's note to parents and teachers: Our editors have reviewed the websites listed here to make sure they're suitable for students. However, websites may change frequently. Please note that students should always be supervised when they access the internet.

INDEX

A
aquariums, 22
attacks, 8, 12, 14, 18

B
batoids, 5, 10, 11, 16
bony fish, 5, 27

C
carrion, 8, 9, 13, 14, 15
caudal fins, 4
cephalopods, 5, 22, 23
continental shelf, 5
cookie-cutter shark, 18
crustaceans, 5, 8, 9, 12, 13, 22, 23, 27

D
dorsal fins, 4, 8, 10, 14

K
krill, 7, 16, 17, 18, 19, 25

M
mollusks, 5, 27

P
parasites, 6, 14
pectoral fins, 4, 16
pelvic fin, 4
plankton, 6, 7, 16, 17, 18, 19, 24, 25
poles, 10

R
reefs, 10, 24, 26

S
stingrays, 10

U
uterine cannibalism, 5, 6, 7, 12, 19, 22